NFL ★ TODAY

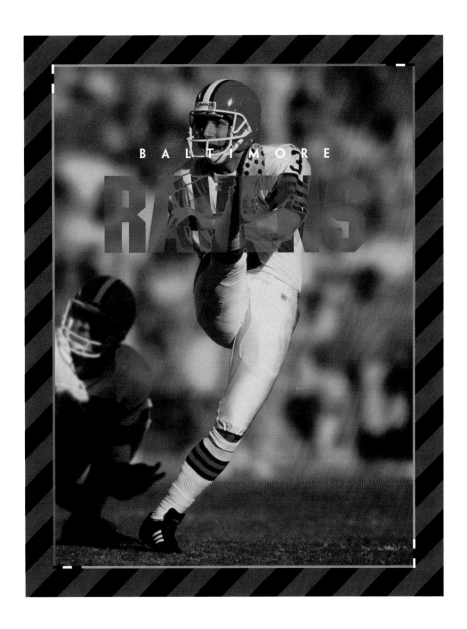

BALTIMORE

LOREN STANLEY

CREATIVE ✦ EDUCATION

Published by Creative Education
123 South Broad Street, Mankato, Minnesota 56001
Creative Education is an imprint of The Creative Company

Designed by Rita Marshall
Cover illustration by Rob Day

Photos by: Allsport Photography, Associated Press, Bettmann Archive,
Focus on Sports, Fotosport, and SportsChrome.

Library of Congress Cataloging-in-Publication Data

Stanley, Loren, 1951-
Baltimore Ravens / by Loren Stanley.
p. cm. — (NFL Today)
Summary: Traces the history of the team from its beginnings through 1996.
ISBN 0-88682-814-7

1. Baltimore Ravens (Football team)—History—Juvenile literature.
[1. Baltimore Ravens (Football team)—History. 2. Football—History.]
I. Title. II. Series.

GV956.C6S83 1996   96-7796
796.332'64'0977132—dc20

9 8 7 6

Baltimore, the largest city in the state of Maryland, is also one of the busiest seaports in the United States. Located on beautiful Chesapeake Bay, Baltimore has been a prominent commercial hub since colonial times. As late as 1850, Baltimore was the second largest metropolis in the entire country, trailing only New York City in population.

Baltimore is known for its bustling harbor, but it has also played a major role in American history. Francis Scott Key composed the "Star-Spangled Banner," our national anthem, at Baltimore's Fort McHenry in 1814. The lyrics to the anthem were inspired by Key's first-hand viewing of a decisive battle

An early Cleveland star, Dub Jones (#86).

The first player signed by the Browns was tailback and future Hall of Famer Otto Graham.

during the War of 1812, when the British fleet bombarded the fort in an unsuccessful attempt to capture it—and Baltimore along with it.

Another part of Baltimore's rich historical tradition is its famous sports teams. In major league baseball, the Baltimore Orioles have been one of the most competitive franchises in the American League for over three decades. In the National Football League, the old Baltimore Colts were one of the great teams from 1953 until 1984—when they moved to Indianapolis.

That move broke the hearts of Baltimore football fans. But then, in late 1995, they received the good news that the NFL was returning to Baltimore. The Cleveland Browns announced that the team would become the Baltimore Ravens for the 1996 season—and would occupy a new football stadium to be built near Oriole Park at Camden Yards, the state-of-the-art baseball complex. The new head coach of the Ravens would be Ted Marchibroda, who had guided the Baltimore Colts to three American Football Conference (AFC) Eastern Division championships in the 1970s.

Baltimore fans now have good reason to celebrate. Their new football team is as rich in tradition as is their city. The former Cleveland Browns have played a great role in the history of pro football. Since 1946 Cleveland was home to a pro football team that was, with rare exceptions, a consistent winner in the NFL. The Browns were named after their first coach, Paul Brown, the man who built the team into a championship franchise.

A Cleveland winner, linebacker Clay Matthews (page 7).

In his debut NFL season, quarterback Otto Graham completed 54.2 percent of his passes.

The Cleveland Browns played their first season in 1946. However, they didn't play in the NFL; they were members of the brand-new All-American Football Conference. The Browns were the only champions in the four-year history of the league. After Cleveland's fourth consecutive championship in 1949, the AAFC's best teams were accepted into the NFL. As good as the Browns had been in the AAFC, no one expected them to be one of the top teams in the NFL. "You're in a real league now," NFL people told the Browns.

But Paul Brown knew his team could play with anybody, mainly because the Browns had a quarterback who was as good as anyone in the game. Otto Graham began his pro football career as a rookie with the Browns in 1946. Unlike other quarterbacks at that time, Graham didn't call the plays on the field. Paul Brown sent in messengers, usually offensive guards, with the calls. Even so, Graham said he had a lot to do with what plays the Browns ran.

"I believe the fellows playing pro ball were actually playing coaches," Graham said. "They know a lot better than anyone else what they can do at a given moment. There were times when I ignored Paul's calls. When my plays worked, he didn't say much. When they didn't, he let me know about it."

The first game the Browns ever played in the NFL was against the Philadelphia Eagles in 1950. Because the Eagles had won the NFL title in 1949, it was a matchup of the champions of the AAFC against the champions of the NFL. More than 70,000 Eagles fans jammed Philadelphia's Franklin Field. The Philadelphia fans expected their team to show Cleveland who the real champs were. But Graham, fullback Marion Motley, and receiver Dante Lavelli put on quite a show. They defeated the Eagles 35-10.

The Browns' success continued throughout their first season in the NFL. They wound up winning the league title in 1950, the team's fifth straight championship but first in the NFL. Cleveland also made it to the championship game in 1951, but the Los Angeles Rams beat the Browns 24-17. For the first time in their history, the Browns weren't champions. "I let you down, Paul," Graham said to his coach after the loss to Los Angeles. "It's part of living," Brown replied. "Nothing to do now but forget it and start thinking of next season."

1 9 5 0

Placekicker Lou Groza was one of seven Browns named to the Pro Bowl.

Led by Graham, the Browns continued to claim division titles, winning in both 1952 and 1953. But they lost the NFL championship to Detroit both times. Despite those setbacks, the team remained confident, which it had every reason to be. No team had more offensive talent than the Browns. Graham had two great pass catchers, Dante Lavelli and Mac Speedie. The running game was led by Dub Jones and Marion Motley, a 240-pound fullback who was bigger than almost all of the linemen. And when the Browns couldn't get the ball in the end zone, they would call on legendary placekicker Lou "The Toe" Groza to boot field goals.

But the key was Graham. The Browns believed that if he was on the field, the team could not be defeated. Against San Francisco in a 1953 game, Graham was sent to the sidelines by a vicious hit. Still groggy, he returned in the second half to complete nine of his last ten passes as Cleveland rallied to win 23-21.

At the beginning of the 1954 season, something strange

Wide receiver Webster Slaughter (pages 10-11).

Fullback Marion Motley (#76) rushed for 444 Yards.

happened to the Browns. They started the year by losing two of their first three games. For the first time in their nine-year history, the Browns were in danger of not playing in the championship game at the end of a season. But Graham pulled the team together, and Cleveland won all but one of its remaining games. For the fourth year in a row, the Browns were Eastern Division champions. For the third year in a row, the opponent in the NFL title game was the Detroit Lions, who had won the league championship in 1952 and 1953. This year, though, the Browns did not wind up second best.

Playing perhaps his finest game as a professional, Graham completed nine of twelve passes for 163 yards and three touchdowns. He scored three more times on runs. As the clock ticked down, Paul Brown took Graham out of the game. The 80,000 fans in Cleveland's Municipal Stadium stood on their feet and

roared for Graham. Behind the strength of his efforts Cleveland won 56-10.

In the locker room after the game, Graham announced he was retiring. "You've got to quit sometime, and it's great to quit while you're on top," he commented.

When training camp started before the 1955 season, Paul Brown tried to find a new quarterback, but no one in camp was as good as Graham. One day, Brown went back to his office and called Graham. "We need you," Brown urged. Graham a-greed to return.

Veteran Otto Graham was a Pro Bowl selection for the fifth consecutive season.

Led by the 34-year-old Graham, the Browns rolled to anoth-er division title, their tenth in 10 years. In the NFL title game, Graham led the Browns to a 38-14 victory over the Los Angeles Rams. "Graham is the greatest ever to play the quarterback posi-tion in pro football," an excited Brown said after the game. A newspaper reporter asked Brown if he would try to get Graham to play again in 1956. "No," Brown answered. "I imposed on him once, and that's enough."

After Graham retired, Cleveland fans wondered where the team would find its next superstar, and when it would find him. As it turned out, it took one year.

A GREAT BROWN, BESIDES PAUL, FOR THE BROWNS

In the 1957 draft, the Browns selected Syracuse University running back Jim Brown, who became a star in his rookie year. The six-foot, 228-pound Brown ran over tackler after tack-ler. "One thing that helps me is my winning style," Brown said. "I don't go into the line in the traditional fullback manner. You don't find me leading with my head. Most of the time the con-

Wide receiver Gary Collins grabbed 43 passes and averaged 15.7 yards per catch.

tact is only my shoulder pads. Normally, I start with small steps so I'll be able to turn or slide toward the opening. When a tackler comes at me, I drop the shoulder. The runner's shoulder should be the first thing to hit the tackler."

The Browns knew they had a weapon in Brown. He was almost indestructible, but some fans wondered if the Browns were using their star fullback too much. After one game, a reporter asked Jim Brown if he was getting too much work. After all, the reporter commented, Brown had carried the ball 34 times in the game. Brown looked the reporter squarely in the eye and said, "If he [Paul Brown] says carry 50 times, then I carry 50 times."

But unlike Otto Graham, Jim Brown didn't have much luck leading the Cleveland Browns to a championship. He was the NFL's leading rusher almost every year, but the Browns never found themselves at the top. In 1962, new Browns' owner Art Modell fired Paul Brown. New coach Blanton Collier worked to develop a good relationship with Jim Brown. His efforts paid off.

The Browns were talking about winning a championship in 1964. In addition to Jim Brown's running game, Cleveland had developed a fine passing attack. Quarterback Frank Ryan had two excellent receivers, sure-handed Gary Collins and speedy Paul Warfield, whose smooth stride resembled that of an antelope. The defense was built around Doug Atkins, an end who would be elected to the Pro Football Hall of Fame.

The Browns spent most of the 1964 season in first place, but a late-season loss to the St. Louis Cardinals damaged Cleveland's title hopes. The Browns regrouped, however, and won their final game of the regular season 52-20 over the New York Giants. That victory enabled Cleveland to finish just ahead of the Cardinals in the Eastern Division. Brown had once again run wild to move Cleveland into the playoffs.

Jim Brown was a league-leading rusher in the 1960s.

Browns quarterback Frank Ryan led the NFL with 25 touchdown passes—a new club record.

"The thing that stands out unforgettably in my mind is his attitude," Cleveland assistant coach Dub Jones said of Brown. "After we lost to the Cardinals, he showed me he was a man. Usually, when the walls start crumbling, the weaker men crumble with them. He helped mend the walls. He did a great job of attitude rebuilding."

Jim Brown and Cleveland weren't through. They faced the Baltimore Colts in the championship game at Cleveland. The game was scoreless at halftime, but the Browns came out in the second half determined to claim their first league title since 1955. Brown gained 114 yards on 27 carries, with most of those yards coming in the second half. Frank Ryan connected with Gary Collins on a couple of scoring passes. Behind these fine contributions the Browns rolled to a 27-0 victory.

Afterwards, reporters asked Jim Brown what the turning point of the game was. "When we held them scoreless in the first half," Brown said, "we proved to ourselves they were human, not supermen. There was pleasure in knowing we could give them a hard time, fight them toe-to-toe."

After the 1965 season, Brown shocked the football world by retiring. He was only 30 years old and had several good years left in him. But Brown said the football part of his life was over. Jim Brown left the game as the NFL's all-time leading rusher. It would take 20 years before another running back, Chicago's Walter Payton, would break Brown's yardage record.

After Brown retired, Cleveland kept on winning, thanks to running back Leroy Kelly and quarterbacks Frank Ryan and Bill Nelsen. In 1970, when the American Football League and National Football League merged, the Browns were moved to the Central Division of the American Football Conference. Other

Quarterback Frank Ryan made the Pro Bowl in 1965.

teams in the division included Pittsburgh, Houston, and the Browns' archrivals, the Cincinnati Bengals. During the early 1970s, both Pittsburgh and Cincinnati built powerful teams. The Browns slumped to third in the division. Owner Art Modell needed to find someone to bring winning ways to Cleveland.

1 9 7 1

Halfback Leroy Kelly (#44) rushed for ten touchdowns.

BRIAN SIPE AND THE KARDIAC KIDS

In 1978, Modell hired Sam Rutigliano to replace Forrest Gregg as head coach. Rutigliano built his team around a quarterback who wasn't very tall and who didn't have a very strong arm. But Rutigliano saw something special in Brian Sipe's attitude. "Brian had been supercompetitive since he was a little kid," Rutigliano said. "I loved it. Don Coryell, who coached Brian in college, told me, 'He'll battle for you.'"

Sipe struggled at times during the 1978 season. Some of the Cleveland fans began booing him and demanding another quarterback. But Rutigliano stayed with Sipe. And eventually, Sipe and the Browns started to get better. They went 8-8 in 1978 and 9-7 in 1979, just missing the playoffs. In 1979 the Browns won seven games with fourth-quarter heroics. The team became known as the "Kardiac Kids" because of its heart-stopping finishes.

In 1980, Sipe and the Browns put it all together. They won the AFC Central Division title and secured home-field advantage throughout the AFC playoffs. Any team trying to prevent the Browns from getting into the Super Bowl would have to win in cold, windy Cleveland Municipal Stadium. The Oakland Raiders came to Cleveland hoping to do just that.

Late in the game, the Raiders had a 14-12 lead. Deep in Raider territory, Sipe went back to pass. He scrambled, nearly fell, and then threw. But the ball went into the hands of Oakland's Mike Davis. After the interception, Rutigliano put his arms around Sipe and said, "Brian, I love you. You had a great year. I know how tough this is for you, but you gotta put it behind you." Oakland won 14-12 and went on to claim the Super Bowl title.

Unfortunately, the Kardiac Kids had reached their peak. The outcome of the 1980 playoffs haunted the team. After the 1983 season, Sipe jumped to the new United States Football League. Rutigliano was fired after the 1984 season. The new coach was Marty Schottenheimer. And the new quarterback was a young star who had grown up near Cleveland. Bernie Kosar went to the University of Miami in Florida, but when he graduated, Kosar said he wanted to play for one team and only one team—the Cleveland Browns.

Browns quarterback Brian Sipe set a new club record with 30 touchdown passes.

Bernie Kosar was a powerful force on the field.

Kosar got his wish when the Browns picked him in the 1985 NFL Supplemental Draft. When he arrived at the Browns training camp, Kosar immediately impressed his teammates with his intelligence and leadership abilities. He became a starter right away.

Kosar combined intelligence with a deadly accuracy. "He knows the game," said Phoenix Cardinals guard Joe Bostic. "He knows what's going on. He says, 'Ball, go here.'" But what amazed people about Kosar wasn't his ability to throw the ball wherever he wanted to throw it; it was the *way* he threw the ball that was unique. "He throws sidearm, underhand, submarine, spitball, slider, knuckleball, and that's only in our first possession," joked owner Art Modell. "But you know what? He gets it there."

Kosar and the Browns became the top team in the AFC's Central Division. The offense was effective in the air, thanks to Kosar and receivers Webster Slaughter, Brian Brennan, and Ozzie Newsome, and on the ground, with running backs Kevin Mack and Ernest Byner carrying the load. Cornerbacks Frank Minnifield and Hanford Dixon were both Pro Bowl selections on defense, but veteran linebacker Clay Matthews might have been Cleveland's best all-round defender.

Behind these stars in 1986, Cleveland posted the best record in the AFC, 12-4. But in their first playoff game, the Browns fell behind the upset-minded New York Jets. Late in the contest, New York's Mark Gastineau was called for roughing the passer when he crashed into Kosar well after the Cleveland quarterback released the ball. Kosar got up and was more determined than ever to rally the Browns. "I saw a look in his eyes I'd never seen before," remembered Ozzie Newsome. "He was

1 9 8 5

Tight end Ozzie Newsome led the club with 62 catches and 711 receiving yards.

23

Left to right: Bernie Kosar, Kevin Mack, Webster Slaughter, Ernest Byner.

not going to be denied. He was going to find a way to win that football game."

And Kosar did find a way. With the Browns trailing 20-10, Kosar engineered two long drives. The first one produced a touchdown and the second a game-tying field goal. The Browns wound up winning 23-20 in overtime.

The following week in Cleveland, Kosar and the Browns needed to beat the Denver Broncos to earn a spot in the Super Bowl. Late in the fourth quarter, Kosar hit Brian Brennan on a long touchdown pass, and the Browns led 20-13. But the Broncos, behind quarterback John Elway, drove to a tying touchdown with less than a minute left. Denver won the game in overtime with a field goal, 23-20, disappointing more than eighty thousand fans in Cleveland Municipal Stadium.

1 9 8 6

Wide receiver Brian Brennan snared 55 passes.

The Browns claimed the Central Division title again in 1987 and advanced to the AFC title game to meet, once again, the Denver Broncos. This time, the game was in Denver. And this time, it was the Broncos who took the early lead. Denver built its advantage to 31-10 in the third quarter, but then Kosar went to work. Cleveland scored three touchdowns to tie the game 31-31. Elway rebounded and led the Broncos on a scoring drive to make the score 38-31. But the Browns didn't quit. "There are no quitters on this team," Kosar said after the game. Kosar moved the Browns to the shadow of Denver's goal line, but a fumble ended Cleveland's dreams of a Super Bowl.

Even though the Browns lost, people couldn't stop talking about how good Kosar had been. Kosar was a star, and everybody knew it. But Bernie just wanted to be one of the guys. "That's what he is, a normal kid from anybody's neighborhood," remarked Cleveland tackle Paul Farren. But this kid had

Brian Brennan had a keen eye for Bernie Kosar's passes (pages 26-27).

exceptional ability, and there was no denying how much he meant to the Browns. "I'd rather blend in," Kosar said. "It's impossible because I'm the quarterback, I know. But I'd like to."

Led by Kosar, the Browns became one of the top teams in the AFC. A new coach, Bud Carson nearly led Cleveland to the Super Bowl in 1989, his first year as the Browns' head man. For the third time in four years, Cleveland met Denver in the conference title game. Unfortunately, for the third time in four years, the Broncos beat the Browns and advanced to the Super Bowl.

1 9 9 6

Lee Roy Hoard once again anchored the Browns' backfield.

REBUILDING IN THE '90s

The Browns were hopeful that a new decade would mean a new milestone for the team—its first Super Bowl appearance. Instead, things took a backwards turn in 1990, with the Browns plummeting to a 3-13 record. For 1991, owner Art Modell was determined to find a new head coach.

His choice was Bill Belichick, who had been defensive coordinator for the New York Giants. Belichick's blunt honesty impressed Modell. When interviewing for the job, Belichick declared that the reason for the Browns' decline was that "your team has gotten old in a hurry and it's not very good." Belichick believed he could turn things around.

The Browns plodded through three more losing seasons. But Belichick delivered in 1994 when the Browns posted an 11-5 record and earned a Wild Card spot. They beat New England 20-13 in the first round before falling 29-9 to the Pittsburgh Steelers.

Their on-the-field leader was quarterback Vinny Testaverde, who had struggled as a pro after winning the Heisman Trophy

Vinny Testaverde had a high pass completion record.

Eric Turner led the NFL with nine interceptions in 1994.

Powerhouse wide receiver, Derrick Alexander.

Veteran coach Ted Marchibroda is sure to lead the Ravens to winning ways.

as a collegiate player in 1986. But 1994 was a breakthrough year for Testaverde. As Browns teammate Rob Burnett said, "He's as talented as any quarterback in the league. I know he's had some tough days, but people tend to overlook his good days."

Testaverde had another solid season in 1995, but publicity surrounding the move to Baltimore disrupted the team's focus. The Browns fell to 5-11, and after the season ended, Belichick was replaced by Ted Marchibroda. Marchibroda was a fitting choice to lead the Baltimore Ravens, as he had successfully guided the Baltimore Colts to winning ways back in the 1970s.

An exciting era is underway in Baltimore. The Ravens have talented players and a proven veteran coach. The 1990s may yet see a Super Bowl appearance for the team with the new name and the long, proud tradition.